T°

FOLLOW THE FLICKERING DOWN

THEODORE SHANK

T °

THERA BOOKS

Turlock, California

SAY / SOMETHING

Follow The Flickering Down
Copyright © 2019 by Theodore Shank

Cover photos copyright © Hyland Stevens

Author photograph by Riley Shank

Cover Design by Mona Z. Kraculdy

All rights reserved. No part of this book can be reproduced in any form by any means without written permission. Please address inquiries to the publisher:

Thera Books
1819 Empress Lane
Turlock, CA 95382

www.thetherabooks.com

ISBN: 978-0-578-60065-9
Library of Congress Control Number: 2019953523

A Thera Books First Edition, November 2019

Printed in the United States of America

For Don and Fern Shank and John and Barbara Baggerly

Contents

Words ... 1
Gone ... 2
Far Back in Shadows ... 6
Kim's Poem ... 8
This Moment ... 9
First Day in Europe ... 10
Jazz ... 12
A Phone Call ... 14
Barre Chords ... 16
What Happened to Duane Larson ... 19
Reading ... 20
The Farrier's Song ... 21
Room 2 ... 22
Night in Prague ... 23
East Side Santa Cruz Music Scene ... 24
4:00 a.m. in Nice ... 26
Overdose ... 27
Camp Roberts ... 28
What Lurks ... 30
Head VI ... 32
The Drowning Angels ... 33
The Flag ... 38
A Game of Catch ... 39
Listening ... 41
The Fence ... 42
The Night I Met a Girl with Dirty Blue Hair ... 44
Witness ... 45
El Puentito ... 46
Cliché ... 49
Moving In ... 50
Without ... 51
Talking to Tombstones ... 52
Trick or Treat ... 54
Bald ... 56
Arrival of the Dead-Moon Dogs ... 58

Acknowledgments ... 65

About the Author ... 66

> What are the roots that clutch, what branches grow
> Out of this stony rubbish? Son of man,
> You cannot say, or guess, for you only know
> A heap of broken images ...
> —T.S. Eliot, *The Waste Land*

> All those stories that my dad told me,
> they are just whispers in time ...
> whispers in time, whispers in time,
> moments that just flicker and die.
> —Bad Religion

> The meaning of an episode was not inside, like a kernel, but outside, enveloping the tale which brought it out only as a glow brings out a haze, in the likeness of one of those misty halos that sometimes are made visible by the spectral illumination of moonshine.
> —Joseph Conrad, *Heart of Darkness*

Words

During World War II
My grandfather wrote for Stars and Stripes,
And after the war he wrote for the local newspaper,
A job from which he never fully retired.
He used to tell me that,
For the writer,
"Every word represents a decision."

After my grandfather's funeral
We all went back to his house.
My cousins, aunts, and uncles
Examined rooms,
Opened drawers,
And looked at pictures on the walls.

Very few words were spoken,

If any.

On a small table
Next to the window
In the living room
Rests my grandfather's Underwood typewriter:

> As a young boy,
> When I would spend the night at his house,
> I would sometimes wake
> To the clacking and rattling of this typewriter;
> It was like a song,
> And often it would sing me back to sleep.

I sat down and placed my fingers
On the cold dark keys,
As though I were about to type something.

But I didn't

Gone

Friday, September 22, 1989

Six of us crammed into my 1969 Dodge Coronet and left Santa Cruz. We were on our way to see BL'AST at 924 Gilman St. in Berkeley, windows down, listening to Black Flag, D.I., and Bad Religion on a small portable cassette player.

Just past the High Street exit in Oakland we started arguing about directions, so we pulled off the freeway and tried to read a blurry map taped to a dirty gas station window. Eventually we found the club.

People were scattered everywhere along Gilman St. Some crouched on sidewalks and curbs. Some clustered together in doorways. Some leaned on cars. Cigarette smoke floated in the air, and everyone seemed to be drinking cheap beer, except two mohawk punks in leather jackets sitting on the curb, a liter of Taaka Vodka between them. Their mohawks were down, hanging far below their shoulders. As we stood in line, I remember thinking that this club could never hold all of these people, that if they attempted to charge into this small building something bad would happen. But the line kept moving, pulling us closer to the entrance.

I handed $7.00 to a girl with a shaved head, and we bumped and jostled into the club. A massive wave of heat confronted me, accompanied by an eye-stinging surge of cigarette smoke, so thick that I coughed, but after a few minutes my lungs adapted.

Through the smoke I saw shadowy figures moving on the dim stage, setting up equipment. We tried to move to the edge of the room, away from the crowd, but people, people were everywhere, smoking, eyes glossy, peering towards the stage. I thought about the others outside: were they going to cascade into this already compacted room when the band started?

Every light went out. An abrupt screech of guitar feedback. Someone jumped onto the stage and leaped into the crowd. I saw his foot collide with a girl's head. A flash of fear raced through my rational mind: this was not safe.

But rationality was obliterated when the music burst into the room. The crowd erupted, a blast discordant, a wild sea of flailing arms, twisting torsos, smoke, and sound. Faces flashed, smiling, angry, sweaty, the whole room moving, violent, mad. And as the night evolved most were bruised and many were bloody.

It was a beginning and an end, all happening at once.

And I became part of it. We all did. If you were there, you exploded—it just happened, without thought or consent. At one point I slipped and fell, only to be picked up by what felt like a hundred hands, which then proceeded to shove me in a million directions. But it was glorious, everyone together—a sublime symphony of chaos.

After the show we piled into the car, excited, shouting, but most of all, laughing. We smelled of smoke, sweat, and beer; our ears rang, and some of us had scratches and cuts. But we were elated, blissful.

As I merged onto the freeway the energy in the car slowly waned, peeling off into the night. Eventually everyone in the car fell asleep as I navigated back to Santa Cruz. But just before silence overtook us, a tired, slightly slurred, voice from the backseat called out, "Know what?" I looked in the rear-view mirror. "That was an initiation, man, that was a fucking initiation."

Soon everyone was asleep, and as the empty freeway sprawled before me, I became acutely aware of my hands, gripping the steering wheel.

Sunday, October 15, 1989

A heavily tattooed coworker of mine sat at the break table, reading a book. I looked over his shoulder. "What is that?" I asked. He told me that it was Henry Rollins' new book of poems. *Rollins? The guy who used to sing for Black Flag? Poetry?* "Can I borrow it?" He shook his head and replied that it was on loan from a friend. But I was overcome by a deep desire to read this book, so after work I rode my skateboard to the Capitola Book Cafe.

"Henry who?" the elderly woman asked, peering over her glasses. "No, we don't have anything by him." I rode back to my apartment, scrambled into the Dodge, and drove to Logos bookstore in downtown Santa Cruz.

Logos was crowded and cool. The long-haired man behind the counter shook his head, but paused for a moment, thinking. "Perhaps," he said, "since Rollins used to sing for Flag and now has his own band, maybe Universe Records carries his books." As I was leaving Logos I heard him call out, "Come back if you don't find anything. I have another idea."

Universe also had no books by Rollins, and the man back at Logos told me to try City Lights in San Francisco. "Ferlinghetti carries pretty much everything in terms of poetry."

"What's City Lights and who is Ferlinghetti?" He sipped his coffee and gave me an overview of this bookstore, its founder, and other figures of the Beat generation. I left Logos with a copy of *Howl*, Gregory Corso's *Gasoline*, and the address to City Lights, handwritten on a piece of paper.

Monday, October 16, 1989

Around 11:00 a.m. I put $15.00 of gas into my car, made sure that the radiator was full, and adjusted the alternator so that the belt was not too loose. Large cup of coffee from Dunlap's Donuts in hand, maps to and of San Francisco spread out on the seat next to me, I made my way over Highway 17 and onto the 280. Since the Dodge had no radio and my portable cassette player was out of batteries, the only sounds while I drove were the wind, the traffic around me, and the powerful rumble of the engine, propelling me onward.

Crowded 280 brought me to congested 19th Avenue, and I began creeping deeper into the city. It quickly became too hard to read the map and drive at the same time, so I parked and started walking. Following street signs, referring to my map, I managed to navigate to the intersection of Columbus and Broadway, where I found myself standing in front of City Lights bookstore.

The boards on the stairs that led to the poetry section creaked, and I emerged into a room of poetry. All poetry. The entire room. I ran my fingers across the spines. The names and titles were unfamiliar—but fascinating. Who is Delmore Schwartz and what could *Summer Knowledge* mean? *Lyrical Ballads*? *Flowers of Evil*? *A Season in Hell*? *The Dream Songs*? I found two of Henry Rollins' books and flipped through the pages. The words. The sounds. I looked around to see if anyone was watching. But the room was empty.

Too excited to simply walk back to my car and begin driving home, I sat down on the sidewalk outside City Lights and started reading, the San Francisco breeze swirling around me.

Night had arrived when I opened the door to our apartment. I was alone: my roommates had gone out to the bars. I dropped into the couch and continued reading. My next memory is standing outside, watching the soft grey light of dawn crawl over 41st Avenue. But there was an energy, a vibration in the growing light. And strangely it was warm, something rare for an October dawn.

Tuesday, October 17, 1989, 5:04 p.m.

I heard a low rumble in the distance, and the earthquake struck. Initially, the quake's magnitude was reported at 7.1, its epicenter Loma Prieta, deep in the Santa Cruz Mountains.

Far Back in Shadows

a 1951 Ferguson
rusts in the weeds;

                                          a boy flies a kite
                                          on the hill
                                          above the high school;

                       a father sits alone in his car,
                       in front of the liquor store,
                       on a Tuesday night;

               a girl cries
               in an empty classroom;

a baseball game concludes
on a Saturday afternoon;

                              a pile of dishes waits to be washed
                              in the sink;

                   a shovel
                     leans against a tree;

                   a Bible lingers on a shelf
                   in the garage;

                       a guitar with no strings
                       sings the corner;

a child walks past a bird,
dead on the sidewalk;

and a mother sits alone
at the kitchen table,
while her family

sleeps

Kim's Poem

She arrived unannounced
At my apartment
Around 10:00 p.m.
I had not seen her for about a month.
It was raining,
And water was dripping from her chin.

"I wrote a poem," she said.

We sat down on the porch
And did not talk for a while:
I watched the rain fall;
She looked for cigarettes in her purse,

Found one,

But had no matches,
So she tossed it into the night
And smiled, nervously.

"I usually don't do things like this."

"Like what?"

"Don't act stupid."

Her lower lip was trembling.

"Do you want to read my poem?"

Rain flickered gently in the puddles.

"Sure."

She handed me a folded piece of paper.
I carefully opened it:

My mascara runs like blood

This Moment

In the early morning hours the storm began,
And by the time I was ready for school
The wind and rain were tearing through
The tall redwood trees near our house.
I stood at the kitchen window,
Watching the wild dance of branches and limbs,
Listening to the pounding rain on the roof.

"Will they cancel school, Mom?"

"I don't think so."

We ran outside,
Splashing through the mud and the puddles,
And jumped into our pickup truck.
Water streaked down the windows,
Distorting the outside world.

"Stop," my mother said,

As a burst of wind hurled
A lifetime of heavy raindrops against the windshield.

"Take a picture of this moment in your mind
And we'll remember it in the summer,
When it is hot and dry,
And we are driving down to the beach
To play in the ocean."

She is smiling,
Strands of wet hair sticking to her face

First Day in Europe

I was painfully tired
When we crossed the English Channel.
I blinked my heavy eyes:
The white cliffs of Dover
Emerged from the fog.

We started driving to London:
Farm houses,
Sheep and cows,
Rolling fields of vibrant green and yellow.

I rubbed my eyes
And tried to refocus.

In one field
A throng of children were kicking a ball,
Running towards a goal with no net.
A boy defending the goal
Crouched down in anticipation,
Beneath the overcast sky.

My eyes stung.

In London
The sky cleared,
And bright sunlight fell on the city.

A middle-aged man in a suit sat down
On a park bench
And lit a cigarette.

A woman
On the street corner
Begged for change.

I squinted.

A statute to
"Our Glorious Dead."

We passed a library in Islington,
Figures of Spenser,
Shakespeare, and Milton
Sculpted into stone walls,
Looming high
Above the sidewalk.

I closed my eyes:

Sweet Thames run softly

'Tis not alone my inky cloak

Pandemonium

Jazz

I was eating my lunch
In Mr. Wolters' classroom,
Listening to music,
Surrounded by tubes of paint,
Unfinished canvases,
And sundry art supplies.
Mike, one of my classmates,
Walked in.
He was tall,
Wore 1950s-style
Button-up shirts,
And his black hair
Was always slicked back.
Mr. Wolters said
That he looked like Chet Baker.
But I didn't know who that was.

"What are you listening to?" Mike asked.

"Youth Brigade."
He listened for a few moments:

> *And we'll sink with California,*
> *When it falls into the sea!*

He put on his smock
And began working on his painting.

The next day
Mike handed me
An unmarked cassette.
"What's this?" I asked.
"I'm not going to tell you,
But I want you to go down to the beach
Early in the morning,
When it's still dark.
    Sit near the water,
        And right as the sun's coming up

Put this tape in your Walkman."

The beach was pitch black
When I arrived the next morning,
And I walked across the sand
To where the waves
Were tumbling
In the darkness.
I sat down,
And slowly the night sky
Began turning morning purple.
I slid the cassette into my Walkman
And waited.
The purple horizon melted into grey,
And just as the sun was about
To appear
I pressed play:

> *Softly floating piano notes,*
> *A smooth bass line,*
> *Calm flowing trumpet joins the piano,*
>
> *The crash of a symbol*

The music washed over me
Like warm fluid,
And nine minutes later
The air was bright and alive,
The ocean
Undulating with energy.

"What the hell was that?"
I asked Mike at school
Later that morning.

> "Miles Davis'
>
> > *So What*"

A Phone Call

My grandmother died a few months before I was born.
Her name was Fern.
As I was growing up
I heard many stories about her,
One of which was about the day she died:

She was in the hospital,
And the doctor called my grandfather—
Her time was imminent,
Sooner than expected,

But Fern died before my grandfather arrived.

On a late-summer day
When I was 8 years old
I was helping my grandfather split firewood.
The phone rang in the house,
About 50 yards from where we were working.

"Go answer it please," he commanded.

I sprinted into the house and picked up the receiver:

"May I speak with Fern?"

I stopped breathing
And stared at the wall in front of me
As my heart surged in my chest.

"Hold on."

I sprinted back across the yard.

What do I say? What do I say?

I jumped over a few
Freshly split logs

Resting in the dirt.

"Someone's on the phone."

"Who is it?"

"I don't know."

I watched my grandfather walk slowly across the yard,

Towards the house

Barre Chords

Eliot had a bass guitar in his room, and his mom's boyfriend had taught him how to play one riff, the first few notes of "La Bamba," the Richie Valens song. Since he could play this simple riff, I told him we should start a punk band, and he liked the idea. Eliot made a few phone calls, and soon we found a guitar player.

"What about drums?" I asked.

"I don't know. We'll find someone."

The guitarist's name was Rye, and he was a few years younger than us. He had been in a reggae band and now wanted to get into punk rock. I was a little worried about starting a band with a guy who knew very little about punk rock music. But at that time we had no other options.

We started jamming at Rye's house three times a week, in his bedroom, without a drummer, and before long we had around 8 or 10 songs. Rye could actually play a little, and Eliot was able follow him, but I had no idea how to sing. I tried to make my voice sound like Dez Cadena, Jack "Choke" Kelly, or Ian MacKaye, but that was the easy part: I did not know anything about timing, and when it came to singing in key, I didn't even know what that meant.

But we were making music, and even though we were in Rye's bedroom, without drums, I would put as much power and emotion into my screaming as I could, jumping on and off the bed and ricocheting off the walls. My plan was to mask my lack of singing ability with extreme energy.

We eventually decided to stop playing until we found a drummer.

A few months later Eliot came over to my house. "I have bad news and good news. Bad news is Rye's been playing with some other guys."

"What's the good news?"

"I think I found another guitar player—and a drummer. They are coming over to my place tonight."

That night Eliot and I met Will, who was still in high school, and his friend Jared, who had recently graduated. They were excited to start a band, but there were two problems. First, they were both into heavy metal and had never heard of any of the punk bands Eliot and I were into, and second, they both had just begun to learn their instruments. I took them out to my car, played a few Circle Jerks songs for them, and they agreed that the songs sounded pretty simple. "I can play that," Jared said.

Later that night, standing in Eliot's driveway, we decided to start a band. We just needed a place to practice.

My parents owned a horse ranch about 10 miles outside of town. The ranch had been vacant for a few years, and they agreed to let us practice in an empty room in the barn. It was a strange room, and I asked my dad what it had been used for. "It once stored sperm to inseminate horses," he told me.

In the room the acoustics were so bad that we decided sound proofing was needed. Carpet on the walls sounded like a good idea, so we salvaged several rolls from the dumpster at a carpet store in town. The carpets were filled with staples, and we received many cuts on our hands and arms as we stuffed the dirty shag into our cars. After a day's work the room was ready; it didn't smell that great, but we didn't care.

At first we struggled to come up with riffs and play them together as a band, so songs were out of the question: we just practiced playing single riffs over and over again with me screaming.

When we were ready to start putting songs together, Eliot and I made a few tapes of our favorite bands for Will and Jared to listen to. We joked that we were converting them from metal to punk. It was very exciting as we began writing actual songs and practicing more regularly. Every time we jammed I blew out my voice, but I was learning, and slowly we got better.

After about three months of practicing we had a handful of songs that we could complete without messing up—for the most part.

One night after practice Eliot said that he knew a guy on 26th Avenue who was having a party, and he had invited us to play. We knew that we had a long way to go as a band, but we wanted to perform live, so we accepted the invitation.

They guy throwing the party was very casual, telling us we could come by and play whenever we wanted, so we decided to show up around 9:30, set up our equipment, and start playing around 10:00 or 10:15.

When we arrived, the house was packed with people, as was the back and front yard, and everyone had consumed a significant amount of alcohol. It was so crowded that we could hardly get our equipment inside, and it took us a while to find and make space to set up. When we were finally ready to play, there was no differentiation between us and the people at the party.

About 30 seconds into our first song everyone began shoving and pushing one another. But it was not the usual slam dancing I'd seen and participated in at punk shows: it was more like a drunken wave washing back and forth across the room.

Beer started spilling and several tangled bodies fell into Will, knocking him over. His amp made a loud buzzing noise and started feeding back; it had been knocked over. He got back to his feet, guitar still slung over his shoulder, and pulled two guys off his toppled half-stack. One of the guys punched him, and Jared leaped over his drums and tackled the other guy, who was about to coldcock Will.

Another fight broke out next to Eliot, and I saw his bass headstock pounding people's heads like he was trying to chop his way through the crowd, which surged and pushed me against the front door; it swung open and I stumbled down the front-porch steps. Close behind me tumbled two guys, wrestling vigorously. In an effort to break them up, I grabbed the guy on top and shoved him into a bush; at the same moment the front window shattered, a loud crash punctuating the mayhem.

The police arrived and the party scattered. Some leaped over the backyard fence, some ran down 26th Avenue, and skateboards and bikes darted in every direction. The police managed to arrest a few people, and order was restored. But the party was over.

We never even played a song.

After the cops left and nearly everyone was gone, we went back into the house to retrieve our equipment and assess its damage.

As I helped Jared load his drums into his car, Chris, one of the older guys, a surfer also known as Bear, who dressed like it was still 1977 and preached his personal philosophy of the "regal peasant formula," crept across the yard and into the street, looking up and down 26th Avenue, making sure the cops were gone.

"Radical show, boys," he said,

"Radical."

What Happened to Duane Larson

Duane Larson had not been at school
For about a month.
I didn't know him that well,
But he was in my P.E. class.

Mark and I were walking home from school
A few days before Thanksgiving break,
And he asked if I had heard about
What happened to Duane:

He and a friend were hitchhiking up to Ben Lomand
To buy some pot.
A guy picked them up
And asked if they wanted to party.
They bought a case of beer
And hiked back into the woods.
They were drinking near an old wood pile
And the guy made some sort
Of sexual advance
Towards Duane and his friend.
Duane panicked,
Grabbed a nearby axe,
And drove it into the man's head.

When I heard this,
I suddenly remembered a shot
That Duane had made during a basketball game in P.E.
It was a wild hook shot,
Which fell perfectly through the hoop,
All net.
Duane's face lit up in a huge smile
And he leaped around the court,
Pumping his fists in the air
Like he had just won
The NBA championship

Reading

Sam was an old man
With a bushy white beard and a hunched posture,
Who used to sit in his yard,
Which was full of bushes and weeds,
On a rickety wooden bench,
Smoking cigarettes
And reading,
Old books,
Thick books,
Like the ones you find
Out front of the library
In a box
With a sign reading
free.
And when we would
Ride our bikes by his house
On the way to and from school,
Mark would sometimes yell,

"Hello Socrates!"

The Farrier's Song

Sitting on an upside-down bucket in the barn,
I watch my father work.

With his tongs
He pulls a bar of hot iron
From the forge
And quickly grabs a hammer
From the rack near his anvil.

Metallic arpeggios
Begin echoing through
The mountains,

Like Years,
Thousands of them,

Rattling across the Sky,

Reaching far beyond
The Horizon

Room 2

When I learned that my elementary school was to be demolished,
I drove to see it,
One last time.

I walked inside Room 2,
Empty, save a few broken chairs
And piles of debris.
High on the wall was a hole
Where the clock once hung.
And I stood,
Staring at this

    Hole.

On the first day of 5th grade,
A warm late-August morning,
My mother and I approached
Room 2.

"You know," she said,
"Your father had 5th grade in this same room."

My mother's hand closed
Around the brass doorknob,
Twisted,
And she glanced inside,
At the clock on the wall,
Above the chalkboard:

"It's almost 8:00,

You'd better go"

Night in Prague

Long after midnight
I begin walking
To the Charles Bridge.

Along the way

        I pass several crowded pubs,
            Warm light spilling out
           Across inky sidewalks;

    Closed shops,
        Windows dark,
        Doors locked;

And I pass
    The place

        Of Kafka's birth.

The Charles Bridge is empty,
    The statues reaching
    Into the darkness,
    Faces obscure
    And indistinct.

Then I hear sounds,
A flute,
    A slow
    Austere melody
    Wandering through the night

East Side Santa Cruz Music Scene

Our apartment was above the Opal Cliffs Market, on the corner of 41st Avenue and Portola Drive. From our porch we could look across 41st Avenue at Cliff Cafe, a small breakfast joint where Dan, bass player for Herbert, worked as a cook. And Dan was dating Yarrow, who played drums in Boobie Trap. They lived in a small trailer park on nearby Capitola Avenue.

Next to Cliff Cafe was Freeline Surf Shop where Dave A., drummer for MOCK, worked. And beside Freeline was the Goodwill where Tina worked; she played bass in TNT and was dating Steve, drummer for Herbert.

Above the Goodwill were rundown apartments that according to local lore used to be a brothel. But now it was where Clifford, who used to sing for BL'AST and now sang for Space Boy, and Brenden, who played guitar and sang in IT, lived.

Kitty-corner to our apartment was Pleasure Pizza and Spirits Liquors. Next to Spirits was Frenchy's, an adult video and bookstore, and Skinny McDougal's, a biker bar that had shows on Sunday nights in the winter when business was slow.

And for about six months there was a bar down 41st Avenue, The 41st Yardline, that had shows on Wednesday nights. But they stopped letting bands play after someone threw a chair through a window after a MOCK show and Bear grabbed the microphone and started reciting his wild poetry about the *dangers of conformity* and the *evils of the system*.

And Eliot, one of my roommates, who played bass in our band, was friends with Rich, drummer for Good Riddance, and Tom, who had been in Rood Riddance but now played bass in Fury 66. They were always hanging out in our living room, especially after everyone was done with band practice and Mystery Science Theatre 3000 was on TV.

And Joe, Eliot, and I had a side band that would jam every Monday at 9:00 in our living room, so we called ourselves Monday at 9:00, and we decided to only write 9 songs. Joe used to sing in Schlep, but was now in Fury 66. Monday at 9:00 never played a show.

For a while Eric, whom everyone called Dog, would sleep on our couch on nights when he would make money hustling pool at Fast Eddies. Dog had played guitar in MOCK but was now in Fury 66. He got his nickname from Dave A.: when they were kids Dave had a dog that Eric really liked, so Dave started calling him Dog. And the nickname stuck.

Dog and Tom would eventually leave Fury 66 and start a new band,

Creature. And while Dog was in Creature, Jack Grisham from TSOL asked him to try out for his new band, The Joy Killer.

A few blocks away lived Bill, who had played drums in BL'AST and was now in LAB. One night around 11:00, after we had finished with band practice, Eliot, Will, Jared, and I were sitting in our living room, drinking from 40 oz bottles of Mickey's Malt Liquor, discussing our songs, and Bill walked up the steps to our apartment and knocked on our door. He had something to talk to us about. We offered him a beer and everything was cool.

Out of her small rented house on nearby 19th Avenue Kim put out a fanzine called *Hectic Times*, in which she interviewed bands, reviewed records and demos, and published stories, poems, and drawings from people in the scene. My first published poem was in *Hectic Times*. And people such as Russ from Good Riddance, Rye from Fury 66, Kevin from Fiendmaster Freak, and Yarrow would help her out with the zine.

After we recorded our first demo I called Dave D., Clifford's brother, who played bass in LAB, and asked him to come by and check out our songs. We started listening and after our first song, "Time Gone By," Dave said, "Holy shit, you guys sound like Zeppelin." And I laughed because we sounded nothing like the mighty Led Zeppelin.

But we were a band,

And it was 1992.

4:00 a.m. in Nice

At the edge
Of the Mediterranean
I sit
Beneath the expiring moon,
Observing my thoughts,
Each one
Arriving
And passing,

Until I think about calling home,
Where it should be about 7:00 p.m.,
And talking to her,
Hearing her voice
For the first time
In three weeks.

I find a phone booth
Outside a hotel,
Where earlier in the day
We had watched prostitutes
And men in suits
Enter
And leave,
Enter
And leave.

At that time,
In the bright exposure of day,
I found this very amusing.

But now,
Alone in the dark,
Approaching the shadowy phone booth,
I don't feel like that

Anymore

Overdose

On a cold winter morning
We sat watching large waves
Dangerously collide
With the rocks
Off the end of the jetty.
Dale ran up the beach
With his surfboard.
He was older than us,
In his 20s,
And we all admired
His surfing abilities.

We watched him slide
Through the shore break
With ease,
And within minutes
An ominous mountain of water approached.
Dale turned,

    Caught the wave,
    And drifted down
    The dark face.

Then the wave closed over him
Like a thick curtain,
And he disappeared,

Swallowed by the sea

Camp Roberts

From his seat at the table
The boy could see the old walnut tree
Outside the kitchen window,
Morning sunlight illuminating the green leaves.

His mother slid a plate
Of eggs, toast, and bacon in front of him.

"Did dad leave?" the boy asked.

His mother returned to the kitchen.

"He left early for San Luis. He'll be back tomorrow night."

She picked up a plate
From the sink
And began drying it,
Slowly.

After breakfast
The boy was marching
Across the front yard.

> *The long road*
> *Down to San Luis Obispo,*
> *Through Greenfield,*
> *King City,*
> *Paso Robles,*
> *Templeton.*

He paused.

The crumbling walls
Of Mission San Miguel

The empty barracks
Of Camp Roberts,

Building after building,
Abandoned,
Empty,
Widows deep,
Breathing.

What happened
To the front doors
Of the church?

    "Don't look, Dad," the boy whispered.

"Please don't look."

Back at the house
The boy's mother stood
Before the kitchen window,
Staring out
At the old walnut tree

What Lurks

The boy runs across the edge
Of the crumbling surf,
Alone.
His mother stands and begins
Collapsing
Their umbrella.

"What are you doing, mom?"

"I'm tired of fighting
This wind.
We have to go soon anyway.
Ten minutes, okay?"

"I don't want to."

"I know, me neither."

The boy lowers his head
And walks back to the ocean,
Kicking the sand.

"Five minutes!"

A small wave breaks
And crawls slowly towards the boy.
It stops just short of his toes
And retreats.
He thinks about chasing it,
But instead turns to his mother.

"Mom, do we have to go?"

"Yes."

As they drift off the beach,
The boy considers the ocean behind him,

And thinks about looking back,

One last time

Head VI

Mr. Wolters is delivering a lecture
On various painters,
Their styles
And tendencies,
Accompanied by a slide show:
Brush strokes and colors,

Mood and tone.

It is late November
And our door is open,
Wide open,
Revealing
Clusters of leaves
Rattling across the walkway,
And iron-grey clouds twisting
In the distance,
Our distance.

And Mr. Wolters calmly
Clicks to a new slide,
An image by Francis Bacon,

And begins his analysis

The Drowning Angels

In Memory of Sara Burke
6/28/1972—6/10/2019

The September sun was dropping into the dark waters of the Monterey Bay as I lingered on the steps that rise above the Capitola village, watching solitary figures march slowly off the beach below, perhaps for the last time. A few tourists climbed the stairs and passed me as though I were transparent. I was unable to move, and I didn't know why.

Wandering through the midnight mountains, the wind assaulting the forest, whipping the trees with tremendous violence. Glass shatters somewhere out in the death-skin night. Where do I go?

After about an hour, with evening closing in around me, a figure approached from the shadows. "Hey! How long you been sitting out here?" I turned and saw a girl with a blond mohawk hanging over her left shoulder. She had bright blue eyes and wore large clunky combat boots.
"I live here." She studied me for a few moments.
"I guess you do. When did you cut your hair?"
"A while ago."
"Were you a skinhead?" she asked quickly, boldly.
"No."
"Good. My ex was." Her tone became playful. "Not gonna beat me are you?" Out in the bay the fog was drifting towards us like a procession of ghosts. "Look, I gotta go, but if you're still here later we can keep talking." She smiled, flashing two twisted front teeth, one with a large chip taken out if it. "I'm Samantha. But you can call me Sam."

Those graves are fresh. I am afraid of the sounds coming from the bushes.

When she returned, Sam sat down and stared menacingly into the night. I noticed that her eyes were red and puffy. She was 17 and had been born in Washington D.C. At the age of 14 she ran away, hitchhiked across the country, and ended up living in L.A. with a group of mohawk punks in a squat. After two years her mom found her and brought her home. Then her mom remarried and moved to Oakland, CA where she could live with her new husband and Sam could stay out of trouble, she hoped.

She then asked what had happened to me. As I talked, the fog floated around us and saturated my sentences.

When I finished talking, Sam was watching me as though she had found something. Then she asked if I wanted to go down to the beach the next afternoon with her and her sister.

Three dogs race across an empty field, bathed in moonlight, steamy explosions of breath bursting into the cold air. I think I should hide behind that large rock. There is a house in the distance.

Sam was sitting in the sand, playfully creating a pile of seashells. She smiled and said that she was making a collection to take home. She introduced me to her sister, Jett, who was smoking a cigarette and drinking a 40 oz bottle of King Cobra. I noticed that she had a frightening scar across her neck.

Sam jogged down to the water to wash her feet. I watched her wiggle awkwardly as a small wave washed over her ankles. "Fuckin' cold!" Two young boys played near her, shoveling wet sand into a bucket. They did not pay attention to her. Sam's sister took a drink.

"She likes you."

"We just met yesterday."

"I know, but you should have heard her talking last night. I never seen her this happy. And she's fucking collecting seashells for Christ sake."

"So?"

"I'm telling you, I never seen her like this." She took another drink. "I heard her laugh this morning—Samantha doesn't laugh." Down at the ocean's edge Sam was splashing water on her legs. "If I tell you something, you promise not to say anything?" I did not respond. "She tried to kill herself three months ago."

Sam smiled and held up a shell, the wind blowing her mohawk in a thousand directions.

She finished with her shells and we spent the rest of the afternoon sitting on the sand, watching the late-summer wind whip the ocean into wild white caps. "It looks sad, like thousands of drowning angels," she said pensively. And I felt her words floating out to sea in the salty breeze.

Eventually we were the only ones left on the beach. Sam ran her hand along the side of her head.

"I think you can help me."

"How?"

"You got clippers, for cutting hair?"

"Yes."

"Good. I need a trim. Getting shaggy on the sides."
"When?"
"Tonight. If you want."
"I'd like that."
She rested her head on my shoulder.

I'm slipping in the mud. Black roses wiggle in the grasp of night. Where is the child? We walk up the steps together and the old boards crackle. A pile of bones in front of the door.

When I arrived, Sam was waiting in the kitchen, surrounded by faded and peeling wallpaper. An old cassette player rested on the table. "You like The Dead Boys?" she asked, pressing play. "I'm way into them. These guys were G.G. Allen's favorite band. Someone told me that at his funeral his brother put a Dead Boys tape in a Walkman and put it on G.G. He pressed play just before they closed his coffin and put him in the ground."

We stood for a moment, listening to The Dead Boys.

"Got those clippers?" As she pulled off her sweatshirt, I noticed a jagged scar about 6 inches long on her back; I reached out and ran my finger across it. She looked back at me over her shoulder and smiled. "I'll kick your ass if you go too fast and screw this up."

I glanced into the living room. Someone was watching TV. "Should we go somewhere else? In the bedroom or something?"

"No. Let's do it right here."

This was my first time cutting someone's hair other than my own, and I was nervous. I slowly slid the clippers back and forth across Sam's head. At one point I trembled and came very close to dropping the clippers. Sam laughed and told me to relax. When we finished, I gently ran my fingers through her mohawk. "Do you ever wear it up?"

"We only put them up for something big, like a GBH show. Or we put them up for fights with the skinheads. If you put it up you have to cut it because we did it with resin. Then you gotta regrow it. If your mohawk is up, you're going to battle."

"Wasn't your ex a skinhead?"

"Yes." We were quiet for a few moments. "I'm leaving tomorrow night."

"But I thought you were going to stay here for a while."

"I was. But it's time. We can hang out tomorrow, though. All day. Just us."

Get out! A rusty horseshoe falls into the dust. The slow groan of a forge. Is that a circle in the dirt? Why is that fence leaning so dramatically?

The next morning we decided to go to Universe Records on the other side of town. As we passed the ocean, Sam's mohawk blew like a flag in the wind. At one point, she looked at me and smiled, flashing her tormented front teeth.

At the record store Sam gave me a small Dead Boys pin. She attached it to my sweatshirt and said that we were married—for the day.

Then she wanted to go to the Boardwalk, a beach-side amusement park on the other side of town. When we arrived, she grabbed my hand and led me through the swirling crowd of bodies. "Come on. Let's go see the kids!"

At the far end of the Boardwalk, a cluster of small rides banged and rattled in the hot sun. We saw a little boy so excited that he was running in place and shaking his head back and forth, blond hair flapping wildly.

We sat on a bench and watched for over an hour, laughing at the kids and their wide-eyed excitement.

"Man, they get so amped up about this shit. I could watch it forever. They have no idea how fucked up the world really is," she said.

"Ever wish you could go back?"

"Maybe we should."

"Go back?"

"No, just sit right here, forever."

We finished the day in Capitola, at the top of the stairs, talking and watching the fog approach.

Just after nightfall Sam announced that it was time for her to leave. I asked if she was going back to Oakland. She said yes, that she had something to take care of at her mom's house. We stood for a while, saying nothing. "Try to get ahold of me in about two weeks. I might still be around," she said.

I watched her turn and drift back into the shadows.

"Hey!" I heard her call from the darkness.

"Yeah?"

"Thank you."

Figures are entering the redwood grove. Is someone singing? The sky is deep black. Another storm is coming.

When I tried to contact her, a strange voice responded. It sounded faint and distant. "Samantha? No, she's gone."

"Can I talk to Jett?"

"She's been gone even longer."

In mid-December I returned to the stairs. Out over the ocean heavy rain clouds approached, and the wind tasted like cold metal. The beach below was empty. I sat down at the top of the stairs, slid a Dead Boys tape into an old Walkman, and pressed play.

The Flag

Over by the bike racks
A group of kids sat in the grass.
The girls were crying,
And the boys were trying to comfort them.

"What's going on?" I asked Mark.

"Nathan Longo jumped off the cliff at New Brighton.
They found his body last night."

Nathan and his mother
Lived in a small apartment
A few blocks away from me.
His father was not around.

A few days later Mark and I rode our bikes
To the cliffs
To see where he jumped.
It had just stopped raining,
And the February wind blew stiff and cold.

Twisted into a bush about halfway
Down the 150-foot cliff
Was an American flag,
Dirty and wet.

"This is where he jumped," Mark said,
"His mom threw that flag off."

"Why?"

"I don't know,
Something to do with his dad"

A Game of Catch

The late-afternoon shadows
Were long and wide
When I heard my grandfather
Calling my name.

I ran over to where he was working,
A large clearing
We called the *flat top*.
He handed me
A well-worn baseball glove,
And I slid my hand into the dry leather.

"I found that out in the shop this morning."

On his left hand
He wore a glove that was even older looking
Than the one he handed to me,
And his right hand gripped a ragged ball.
He took a few steps back
And flipped the ball towards me.

The seams were coming apart,

And their frayed tips looked like spider webs
Twisting in the dying light.

I tried to catch the ball,
But missed.

"That's okay. We'll start close, and as you get more comfortable we'll take
   a few steps back."

Soon we were about
Ten yards apart,
The only sound
The soft clapping of the ball colliding with our gloves.

My grandfather's motion
Was fluid and familiar.

Then he stopped,
Held the ball,
And looked around,
At the trees,
The soft summer sky,
The house
In which he lived,
Alone.

"What is it?" I asked.

"Nothing"

Listening

Long before the sun
My father woke.
And sometimes I would also rise,
Turn on our small
Black and white television set,
And watch "Rin Tin Tin"
With the volume low,
So I could hear
The sounds of my father
Making breakfast.

Then before leaving
He would rub my head
And say,

"Have a good day, tiger."

And I would listen,

To his boots
Thumping
Down
The back porch steps;

To the door
Of his truck,
Loudly closing;

To a dog barking
In the distance,

And then to the stillness
Of our house

The Fence

My uncle was living with us
During one of the hottest summers
I can remember.

He and my father had been
Working for days,
Repairing a fence down in the orchard.

Now the sun was falling,

And we were sitting
On the front porch.
Between us sat a small portable radio,
Broadcasting a baseball game.

The 2-1 pitch is low and outside.

The words were slow and loose.
The sun slid behind the redwoods,
And the mountains were warm and still.
On the radio, the game continued.

A fly ball to deep right ... that's two away, and McCovey is coming to the plate.

My uncle stood up.

"Do you want a beer?"

"I don't think we have any."

"I'll check."

He returned with two cans of beer.

McCovey hits a slow roller to short ... the throw to first, and the side is retired.

"I think it's good McCovey's back,"
My father said, holding his beer.

He had yet to take a drink.

I looked at my uncle,
Anticipating his response.
But he said nothing.

Interested, I asked,
"Why did he come back?"

It took a few moments for my father to reply.

"He's getting older. Probably wants to end his career
Where he started."

My uncle slowly sipped his beer.
"Think we can finish that fence tomorrow?" he asked.

"I'm not sure"

The Night I Met a Girl with Dirty Blue Hair

I wanted to see
Live music,
But there were no shows
In Santa Cruz,
So I drove to 924 Gilman,
Where they had shows
Almost every weekend.

I had never heard
Of the bands who were playing,
And hardly anyone
Was at the show,
20 people at the most.

When the first band started,
The small crowd began dancing,

But there was so much space
Between them

And the music,

So I stood by myself,
Listening,
Watching.

And after a few songs
A girl with dirty blue hair
Grabbed my sweatshirt

       And pulled me
       Into a small void

       In the middle of
           Madness

Witness

From a deep sleep
My father summons me
And tells me to quickly get dressed
And follow him to the barn.

Joined by my mother,
We walk together
Through the darkness.

Inside the barn, my father lifts me up
And puts me on the edge of the first stall on the left:
A horse lies on her side.
My father says she is going to

"Throw her foal at any moment."

I watch in silence as the horse gives birth.
I see everything.
My parents say nothing.
But a hand rests on my back,
Steadying me.

When it is finished,
And the mare begins cleaning her foal,
Licking it with her large pink tongue,
My father disappears into the barn,
And my mother tells me

It is time to go back to the house:

I only have a few more hours to sleep
Until I must wake again,

And get ready for school

El Puentito

The summer season had arrived in the small beach town. The boy was sitting in the alley behind El Puentito, a small Mexican restaurant, leaning comfortably against her warm boards. The back door opened, and a young man whom the boy did not recognize stepped into the dusty alley. The boy noticed that across his arms crawled a community of tattoos: Roman numerals, webs, chains, a woman in a fedora, face half-skull, crying. He paused for a moment after tossing a bag into the trash, looked at the boy, and nodded, slightly.

Later in the day, Carlos, the cook and owner of El Puentito, informed the boy that the young man's name was Henry, and that he had hired him for the summer.

The day after the 4th of July the boy was again sitting in the alley, resting in the safety of El Puentito's shadow as she slept in the salty sunlight. Three men in their early 20s walked past the alley.

"Is that him?" one of them asked, pointing at the boy.

El Puentito stirred. Waves and sand clashed on the beach.

"You over by the pier last night?"

"Why?"

"Well after the fireworks someone broke our front window. Saw some kids running toward the pier and one of them looked like you. I think we need to go talk to the cops."

El Puentito moaned.

"I didn't break any windows. It wasn't me."

"Well you can tell that to the cops. Let's go."

The back door opened. Henry stepped between the boy and the accuser.

"What's going on?"

"Look we're from out of town and we're staying over in the rentals. This kid broke our window last night."

Henry looked at the boy. "You do this?"

"No."

Henry shrugged. "Guess we got no problem—amigo."

Silence. A calm intensity glowed in Henry's eyes. One of El Puentito's boards creaked.

"Okay, but I'm filing a report and I'm gonna describe you to the cops." They turned and left the alley. Henry quietly went back to work.

The summer continued rolling through the town, and El Puentito started whispering to the boy. He began anticipating summer's close with increasing trepidation.

On a fog-drenched night in mid-August, the boy returned to the alley. Henry tossed a bag into the trash, sat down, and lit a cigarette. "Something's going on these days. I sense it. You know what it is?" he asked.

"This is a strange time of year. Always feels kind of weird."

"Not like this where I'm from."

"Where are you from?"

"L.A. Boyle Heights." El Puentito reached through the fog and touched the night sky.

"So why did you come here?"

Henry stood and looked pensively into the fog.

"Gotta get back to work." He dropped the half-finished cigarette into the dirt. The boy watched it burn.

As the days passed, the afternoons became thick and uncomfortable. Hot sand. Sweat. Red sunburned skin. El Puentito struggled to breathe.

The evening before Labor Day, during the final moments of daylight, the boy was walking towards El Puentito. The sidewalk was crowded with warm bodies. He watched a group swarm into Mac's Patio, a nearby bar.

Then abruptly a commotion erupted down the sidewalk in front of El Puentito. People screamed. Flesh slapped pavement. The boy ran to investigate.

As he approached, El Puentito's eyes filled with tears. Before her on the sidewalk, Henry was holding a man down, fists slamming into his face. More screaming. The boy recognized the man: he was the one who had accused him of breaking the window on the 4th of July.

El Puentito attempted to reach out for the boy, but she struggled. She was growing weak. Tears rolled down her faded grey boards. Sirens rang in the distance.

Henry darted down the alley and across the beach, towards the pier, disappearing in the shadows below. The boy followed. El Puentito tried again to restrain him. But she failed.

He found Henry sitting in the sand, tears streaking down his face, hands vibrating, blood dripping from his knuckles. "I fucking hate violence. Hate it. But that guy. He just. *Mi hermana*. And. That *pinche* fucking *puto*." He covered his face with his hands.

The boy sat down and listened to Henry cry. He eventually stood and walked away.

El Puentito closed her eyes and exhaled.

The next morning the boy raced to El Puentito. Through the back door he saw Carlos, alone.

"Have you seen Henry?" the boy asked.

"No. Cops just left though."

"Cops?"

"Yeah, they're trying to figure out what happened last night. I told them what I saw. That guy was out front of Mac's Patio, drunk, and he got into an argument with a girl. It looked like he was going to hit her. He was really being an asshole. Henry saw it too and ran outside, said something about protecting her. The guy took a swing at Henry and that was it. Henry messed him up pretty good."

"Where is he now?"

"Don't know. Cops are looking for him though. They talked on their radios then they said they know who he is. They were on their radios for quite a while."

The boy felt a surge of anger, but El Puentito was as still and quiet as a corpse.

Cliché

On My 21st Birthday

I pinned a towel
Over my bedroom window

So that minimal
Light could enter,

Slid Minor Threat's
"Out of Step"
From its sleeve,

Carefully placed
The black vinyl
On the turntable,

And listened to
Ian MacKaye

Scream in
The darkness

Moving In

I had just moved into my first apartment
With two friends,
Who were also my bandmates.

I was sitting on the couch
We bought at the Goodwill
Across the street,
Reading.

Pete Richmond walked in
The open front door.
Pete was about 5 years older than me,
And he had been in several
Local bands.

"Heard you guys moved in here.

    Welcome to the neighborhood."

"Thanks."

Pete surveyed our living room,
Which contained only the couch
On which I was sitting.

"You know the history of this place, right?"

"Not really, why?"

He lit a cigarette.
"Let's just say
I remember shooting up
Right over there,"
He said, pointing to

An empty corner

Without

A few weeks after I finished 6th grade
My family told me
We were moving
Off the mountain.
After hearing this
I walked out to the porch:

A redtail hawk
Drifted across the sky,
A small rodent
Dangling from its talons.

That evening,
Sitting in my room,
I prayed
For the first time.
I did not ask for anything,
But I wanted God to know

I was leaving the mountain

Talking to Tombstones

Everyone in Art class called him Red Dog
Because of his long red hair.
His favorite bands were
Iron Maiden, Anthrax,
And Megadeath.
And he was a talented artist.

In early October of 1986,
Mr. Wolters took us
To the cemetery
Down the street from our high school
To draw.

Red Dog disappeared
Into the far corner of the cemetery,
And soon a cloud of pot smoke
Rose from behind one of the tombstones.

After a few minutes he emerged from the smoke
And approached a tall tombstone,
Which he grabbed with both hands,
And aggressively began to shake,
Dirty red hair swirling around his face.

"Fuck Jesus!" he yelled,

"Fuck Jesus!"

Mr. Wolters approached
Just as the tombstone was about
To topple.
"What are you doing?"
Red Dog stopped
And flipped his fiery hair from his face:

"I'm sorry, Mr. Wolters."

Then he walked back to the corner

Of the cemetery,
Where a fresh cloud of pot smoke
Drifted into the air,

And began drawing

Trick or Treat

A few days before Halloween
Someone knocked
On our front door;
It was my father.

"You got a minute?" he asked

"Sure."

I waited for him to speak.

Outside on the patio
My boys were cleaning the seeds
And sinew from their pumpkins.

"Do you remember Roger Brown?"

One of my boys
Threw a pumpkin seed at his brother.

"Yes."

I catch three fish in a freezing mountain stream
About 50 yards from camp.
"Know how to clean 'em?" Roger asks.
"No."
He slides his knife from its sheath,
Blade shining brightly in the morning sunlight,
And demonstrates how to
Gut the fish
And remove the organs.
When he finishes,
He hands me the knife:
"Your turn."
I shake my head.

"These fish are already dead, boy."

He stares at me
For what feels like a long time
Before he cleans his knife in the stream,
Dries the blade on his pant leg,
And carefully slides it back into its sheath.

"Well, he died a few days ago."

"How?"

"They aren't too sure yet."

My father left.

I walked into the fading October light
And watched my boys at work,
Carving their pumpkins,

Discussing
Their Halloween

Costumes

Bald

In autumn
Of my final high school year
I grew angry about something,
I can't remember what,
So I shaved my head
Completely bald;
It felt and looked strange
And I regretted doing it,
So I wore a beanie.

As I walked home one afternoon,
A girl named Shae

Crossed to my side of the street.

She had short brown hair,
Olive skin,
And eyes so dark
They could devour you.

"Can I walk with you?"

"Sure."

We passed through the shadows
Of a large elm tree.

"I heard you shaved your head."

"Maybe."

"Can I see?"

"No."

We stopped walking.

"Please?"

Then she cautiously raised her hands,
And I allowed her
To slowly remove my beanie

Arrival of the Dead-Moon Dogs

    I

below the cellophane moon
        flashing lights
        hot iron horizon night
        smoldering sidewalks

soon to awaken
        the dry grass
        the trees
        our sleeping mind marriage of dirt and dust

falling leaves
        she cannot hear the distant symphony

so we twist
race
dance mad brilliant among the tombstones
            singing of the lost
            the father
            the mother
            another day waiting in boxcar dreams

    a child never conceived
        clouds of the cold stomach
        hollow cries

            palms opening across sky
            whispering young

a quiet rattle
from the dying red Sunn

"have you heard about the 2012 predictions?"

II

toes in the dirt
                        stomach burning
      she arrives
      tossing hair imperative
      dense heavy wet sand music

investigation
moist hands slowly gripping
      a face
      a ritual
      the sounds of mourning

eyes lost
      bodies contorting
      songs echo
            "my god, what are you doing to me?"

        dead jazz distortion

        the walls vanish

      vivid colors
      vibrations
      syncopated intervals

        then nothing

black hair tangled
      sprawling across a broken pillow

white coat crumbles
cold bare shoulders

        the animal departs

           looking for another place to die

III

    alone in the back room
            slicing glossy narratives
            sipping on wine box words
                  dirty sunglasses

               laughter roams the backyard bushes

the hot summer swells
feet fire animal tongues
a window softly breaks

the sea in the distance
           waves burn
           sand objects

                salty wash of oceanic night

"where did she go?"

           the neighbors standing
           drinking
           dry knuckles
           empty cans clatter
           smoke roams the air

           fireworks screaming tear open the sky

  her skin
           the loosening grip of gossamer fingers

              "take them off!"

the wine glass slips
and gently tumbles
   into the bloody grass of

    o' say can you see
    by the dawn's early light

IV

trying to stop listening to 4 a.m. walls
                                            overturned couches
                                            children confused in the hall

                                         dirty linoleum
                        discovery
glossy women in dead magazines

                    absent expressions

television ingestion
devastation crossroads of the mind
        voices drifting to silence

        the carpet breathes

she is next to me

                    canyons of dreams

worrying about the stains
on her wedding dress

        looking for more wine

                    this canvas
                    our world
              these drinks
                a slow sullen breeze
                a wandering disease
the final assertion of a hundred good men
the once
the twice
        the everyone calls

                    the lizard-skin ghost walk
                    of 4 a.m. walls

V

"I want to feel again"
she moaned
while memory crawled across our bones

        vacant shadows tumbling inquiry

"do something
        anything"

        a slowly opening wound

    tragic skin crawling warm

desperately redundant

        a decision is made

descend into the
    redwoods

the windows are dirty

    warmth and wetness
    sliding
    skin colliding
        candles
        flames crossing
        shadows

moonlight starvation water

        "was that really you?"

        stumbling naked down the hall

        we fall into the fabric of inebriated night

VI

A cool morning
envelops us,

but it is warm beneath the blankets.

I gently slide
my hand
across her bare shoulders.

She turns away from me.

I remove my hand.

"Have you looked outside? Is it nice out?" she asks.

I toss off the blankets
and look out the window.

"Yes, but there are still a few clouds

out there."

"I hope it clears up."

"Me too."

Francis Bacon, Head VI, 1949
© The Estate of Francis Bacon. All rights reserved, DACS/Artimage 2019.
Photo: Prudence Cuming Associates Ltd

Acknowledgments

"What Happened to Duane Larson" originally appeared in the short story "Capitola, California, 1983" in the 2009 edition of the *Porter Gulch Review*

"The Drowning Angels" originally appeared in the 2011 edition of the *Porter Gulch Review*

Part IV of "Arrival of the Dead-Moon Dogs" originally appeared as "Ghost Walk" in the *Perfume River Poetry Review*, Issue 3: Night Terrors, 2015

"El Puentito" originally appeared in 2017 edition of the *Porter Gulch Review* and won the "Best Prose" award for that edition

"Searching" originally appeared in the 2018 edition of the *Porter Gulch Review*

"A Phone Call" appeared in the 2019 edition of the *Porter Gulch Review*

And a special thanks to Donnelle McGee and Colleen Mills.

About the Author

Theodore Shank's writing has appeared in *Reed Magazine, Porter Gulch Review, Perfume River Poetry Review, Inside Surf* magazine, *The Santa Cruz Sentinel*'s Poetry Space, and *Hectic Times* fanzine. His short story, "El Puentito," won the Best Prose award for the 2017 edition of The Porter Gulch Review. Over the years, in addition to writing, studying literature, and teaching, Shank has been an active member of the Santa Cruz underground music scene. In the early 90s, he was the vocalist for the local rock band Lost in Line, before switching to bass for bands Locus and Time. In the late 90s-early 2000s, he was bassist and founding member of The Fire Sermon, a band that put out 3 records, Burn, Freaks and Healers, and Love Lies Bleeding and performed extensively in the San Francisco Bay Area and on the West Coast. In more recent years, Shank has developed a deep appreciation for Jazz, especially Miles Davis, John Coltrane, Bill Evans, Dave Brubeck, Thelonious Monk, and Charles Mingus. Therefore, music is a major influence on the mood, tone, impressions, and rhythms of his poetry and prose. Shank lives in Capitola, California with his wife Katie and two boys Cooper and Riley. He currently teaches English at Mission College in Santa Clara, California.

About the Press

Thera Books is an independent publishing house based in Turlock, California. We aim to publish writers pushing the boundaries of literature and writing about what it means to be human.

www.thetherabooks.com

www.ingramcontent.com/pod-product-compliance
Lightning Source LLC
Chambersburg PA
CBHW021959290426
44108CB00012B/1139